The Evolution of Attachment

I must confess: I did not love you well

Lahni Pearson

Dear reader this is for you.

Take a moment now before you begin, to take a
break.
Pour yourself a glass of your desired beverage
whether that be tea, coffee, wine or water. whatever
takes your fancy.
Take a seat outside. You will feel more alive.
I hope the words inked onto the following pages
bruise your skin or move you in some way. They
certainly moved me. From the classroom, to my
bed, to sobbing uncontrollably on my bathroom
floor at two in the morning.
You will never be here again and this will never be
more unfamiliar than it is right now.

Our souls danced and we couldn't control it

I ignored every sunset when I was with you

how naive to believe you held the most beauty my eyes
had ever seen

it's a Monday morning and you're too sad to move
there is nothing beautiful about heartbreak
I am not ashamed to say I cried so much yesterday I
woke up with swollen eyes
you don't forget the feeling

    — I will search for you in everyone I meet

I couldn't leave my bed for sixteen hours debilitated by
loss
staring upward at the cracked ceiling that witnessed our
love
needing to bleach the memories from my brain
What changed?
I scream
I burn
I collapse
I can hear my bones break
gravity ripping my heart through my chest
a feeling I swear I wouldn't handle a second time around

Fear welcomed me *what if you're never that happy
again*

Nostalgia whispered in my ear *everything was perfect*

Grief pat me on the back *this isn't how its supposed to
be*

How fast the world spins when you're on top of it

I started hydrating on black coffee and straight whiskey
if it wasn't strong I didn't want it

I began wondering what my veins would look like split
open

I would wake up every night to the ghost of your lips on
mine

I threw out the shirt I was wearing when I first met him
it was my favourite

— look love I can ruin me too

I am wading through our ruins
knee deep in forgotten corpses and collapsed castles

I grew roots in your bones but people are not gardens

Drinking whiskey so strong it burns your throat isn't
going to make you forget the way their lips felt pressed
against yours

Crying yourself to sleep every night isn't going to bring
them back

Marking your skin and yelling at the people you love
isn't going to make you feel better

       — love letter to me from me

Still
I am questioned on why you abandoned me like the dead
plant by your window cill
and still
I find myself suffocating on the words I don't have
ownership of
my sentences trailing off a cliff I haven't jumped from
since I was seven

<u>July</u>

To me July was your favourite playlist on repeat and
perfect toast
Memories of the best Christmas you ever had and
winning uno four times in a row
To me July was getting wasted with your best friends
and falling into the arms of your lover

I was hesitant to remove him from my wall of memories
now there are blank spaces where you should be
I wish photos could talk, that girl looks so happy

    — two months later and I have accepted you're
    not coming back

I have a terrible habit of breaking things I shouldn't
I am never entrusted with the items dear to people
I am destined to damage it every time
tonight my mother yelled at me
*why should you have the best of anything if you're only
going to break it*
out of her mouth stumbled forbidden truths
I screamed at the burning stars
why do I break every thing I touch
its true
every friendship I have held has crumbled down into a
broken mess
its true
at ten years old I popped the wheel off my fathers
remote control car on my first turn
its true
every boy I have let inhabit my life has proven to be
temporary
it was me
I broke us
my hands don't know how to hold something fragile
I'll drop it
I'll drop it every time

I had been craving this exact moment
with you
here
for years
how come his hand in mine still dances on my mind
I lace my fingers through yours choking up memories of
when I was here
here with him

I still search for him in cities of lust and skies of manipulation

So ill jump from distraction to distraction from
attachment to attachment
self medicating on alcohol and sex
but I no longer need anyone to fuck me as hard as I
hated myself
impostors for the love only I can provide

But here is the thing about timing

Its rarely in our favour and when it is
we ignore it

You salivate over my naked body like an animal begging
to feast
you're starving
your deprived body convinces you I am exactly what you
need
that I will fill you in all the ways you need to be filled
you feast upon my exposed skin
no longer drunk off starvation
realisation hits you hard in the chest
I am not what you want
I will not fill you in all the ways you need to be filled
the high has worn off
my naked body is no longer calling you in
you can see clearly
I am not worth the calories

Oh young innocent me
there is so much I need to warn you about and yet... tragically
I can not

Notice when things reach their expiry
wether this be chocolate milk or friendships. Don't be afraid to
let go
there is almost always going to be someone better
a better friend a better lover a better postman. Don't settle
if you're going to fall in love don't linger on the edge waiting
on someone to push you in. Fall. Fall headfirst and
wholeheartedly
let it consume you
if your going to fall in love let it ruin you too
but understand when it is time to pick yourself back up again
and when you find something that makes you feel alive
pursue it at all costs
take exquisite care of yourself
you are the only one you will ever have to spend the rest of
your life with
you are a product of the five people you spend most of your
time with
take this very personally
this is all so very arbitrary
you don't have to make sense of it to enjoy it
do what you want
also do what is right
your gut instincts won't lie like your head will
never do anything at the expense of yourself
realise everything must eventually come to an end
enjoy where you are now
you cant fight the moving of time
move with it
allow your heart too as well
commit absurd acts in the name of living
if something doesn't feel good
stop it
whether this be drinking milk or sex
listen intently to your body

you don't know me anymore
my nails have grown and my hair is cut
I don't wear those dirty nikes and I have discovered a
new taste in music
the friends I would tell you about are now strangers
and I have more hobbies then just you
I have outgrown me and certainly outgrown you

<u>If asked to describe him</u>

I would tell them he is the third time I tried to quit
smoking
I would tell them he is the tile floor my favourite mug
shattered upon
I would tell them he is new years day and the smell of
burnt sparklers
I would tell them he is orange juice after brushing your
teeth
I would tell them he is insomniac nights
I would tell them he is afternoon rain and the two
dollars you find at the bottom of the washing machine
I would tell them he is every sunrise in human form
I would tell them he is praying to a god that doesn't exist
I would tell them hearts don't break they bruise and get
better
I would tell them he is the thirteenth shot of vodka
I would tell them I can now admire the blueness of the
sky and not be shot with him

These holidays I worked myself until bare flesh and bone
were showing

I am so constantly hungry sometimes I feel as if I am
nothing but ache

I threw anything that didn't serve me current purpose
into the garbage

These holidays I drank tequila every night in celebration

I beat the sun up every morning to countdown her
arrival

I haven't spoken to most of my friends since school
ended

I know it doesn't sound like it

But this is a love poem

This is a love poem

This is a love poem